Do not think you have to say
Anything back. But you do
Say something back which I
Hear by the way I speak to you.

W. S. Graham, from 'Implements in their Places'

Denise Riley

Say Something Back

PICADOR

First published 2016 by Picador
an imprint of Pan Macmillan
20 New Wharf Road, London N 1 9RR
Associated companies throughout the world
www.panmacmillan.com

ISBN 978-1-4472-7037-9

1 3 5 7 9 8 6 4 2

A CIP catalogue record for this book is available from the British Library.

Printed and bound by CPI Group (UK) Ltd, Croydon, CR0 4YY

For my friends, and for my children:

Rose, Laura, and remembering Jacob

Contents

Say Something Back

Maybe; maybe not

When I was a child I spoke as a thrush, I
thought as a clod, I understood as a stone,
but when I became a man I put away
plain things for lustrous, yet to this day
squat under hooves for kindness where
fetlocks stream with mud – shall I never
get it clear, down in the soily waters.

A Part Song

You principle of song, what are you *for* now
Perking up under any spasmodic light
To trot out your shadowed warblings?

Mince, slight pillar. And sleek down
Your furriness. Slim as a whippy wire
Shall be your hope, and ultraflexible.

Flap thinly, sheet of beaten tin
That won't affectionately plump up
More cushioned and receptive lays.

But little song, don't so instruct yourself
For none are hanging around to hear you.
They have gone bustling or stumbling well away.

ii

What is the first duty of a mother to a child?
At least to keep the wretched thing alive – Band
Of fierce cicadas, stop this shrilling.

My daughter lightly leaves our house.
The thought rears up: *fix in your mind this*
Maybe final glimpse of her. Yes, lightning could.

I make this note of dread, I register it.
Neither my note nor my critique of it
Will save us one iota. I know it. And.

iii

Maybe a retouched photograph or memory,
This beaming one with his striped snake-belt
And eczema scabs, but either way it's framed,
Glassed in, breathed hard on, and curated.
It's odd how boys live so much in their knees.
Then both of us had nothing. You lacked guile
And were transparent, easy, which felt natural.

iv

Each child gets cannibalised by its years.
It was a man who died, and in him died
The large-eyed boy, then the teen peacock
In the unremarked placid self-devouring
That makes up being alive. But all at once
Those natural overlaps got cut, then shuffled
Tight in a block, their layers patted square.

v

It's late. And it always will be late.
Your small monument's atop its hillock
Set with pennants that slap, slap, over the soil.
Here's a denatured thing, whose one eye rummages
Into the mound, her other eye swivelled straight up:
A short while only, then I come, she carols – but is only
A fat-lot-of-good mother with a pointless alibi: 'I didn't
Know.' Yet might there still be some part for me
To play upon this lovely earth? Say. Or
Say *No*, earth at my inner ear.

vi

A wardrobe gapes, a mourner tries
Her several styles of howling-guise:

You'd rather not, yet you must go
Briskly around on beaming show.

A soft black gown with pearl corsage
Won't assuage your smashed ménage.

It suits you as you are so pale.
Still, do not get that saffron veil.

Your dead don't want you lying flat.
There'll soon be time enough for that.

vii

Oh my dead son you daft bugger
This is one glum mum. Come home I tell you
And end this tasteless melodrama – quit
Playing dead at all, by now it's well beyond
A joke, but your humour never got cruel
Like this. Give over, you indifferent lad,
Take pity on your two bruised sisters. For
Didn't we love you. As we do. But by now
We're bored with our unproductive love,
And infinitely more bored by your staying dead
Which can hardly interest you much, either.

viii

Here I sit poleaxed, stunned by your vanishing
As you practise your charm in the underworld
Airily flirting with Persephone. Not so *hard*
To imagine what her mother *had gone through*
To be ferreting around those dark sweet halls.

ix

They'd sworn to stay for ever but they went
Or else I went – then concentrated hard
On the puzzle of what it ever truly *meant*
For someone to be here then, just like that,
To not. Training in mild loss was useless
Given the final thing. And me lamentably
Slow to 'take it in' – far better toss it out,
How should I take in such a bad idea. No,
I'll stick it out instead for presence. If my
Exquisite hope can wrench you right back
Here, resigned boy, do let it as I'm waiting.

X

I can't get sold on reincarnating you
As those bloody 'gentle showers of rain'
Or in 'fields of ripening grain' – oooh
Anodyne – nor yet on shadowing you
In the hope of eventually pinpointing
You bemused among the *flocking souls*
Clustered like bats, as all thronged gibbering
Dusk-veiled – nor in modern creepiness.
Lighthearted presence, be bodied forth
Straightforwardly. Lounge again under
The sturdy sun you'd loved to bake in.
Even ten seconds' worth of a sighting
Of you would help me get through
This better. With a camera running.

xi

Ardent bee, still you go blundering
With downy saddlebags stuffed tight
All over the fuchsia's drop earrings.
I'll cry 'Oh bee!' to you, instead –
Since my own dead, apostrophised,
Keep mute as this clear garnet glaze
You're bumping into. Blind diligence,
Bee, or idiocy – this banging on and on
Against such shiny crimson unresponse.

xii

Outgoing soul, I try to catch
You calling over the distances
Though your voice is echoey,

Maybe tuned out by the noise
Rolling through me – or is it
You orchestrating that now,

Who'd laugh at the thought
Of me being sung in by you
And being kindly dictated to.

It's not like hearing you live was.
It is what you're saying in me
Of what is left, gaily affirming.

xiii

Flat on a cliff I inch toward its edge
Then scrutinise the chopped-up sea
Where gannets' ivory helmet skulls
Crash down in tiny plumes of white
To vivify the languid afternoon –
Pressed round my fingertips are spikes
And papery calyx frills of fading thrift
That men call sea pinks – so I can take
A studied joy in natural separateness.
And I shan't fabricate some nodding:
'She's off again somewhere, a good sign.
By now, she must have got over it.'

xiv

Dun blur of this evening's lurch to
Eventual navy night. Yet another
Night, day, night, over and over.
I so want to join you.

xv

The flaws in suicide are clear
Apart from causing bother
To those alive who hold us dear
We could miss one another
We might be trapped eternally
Oblivious to each other
One crying *Where are you, my child*
The other calling *Mother*.

xvi

Dead, keep me company
That sears like titanium
Compacted in the pale
Blaze of living on alone.

xvii

Suspended in unsparing light
The sloping gull arrests its curl
The glassy sea is hardened waves
Its waters lean through shining air
Yet never crash but hold their arc
Hung rigidly in glaucous ropes
Muscled and gleaming. All that
Should flow is sealed, is poised
In implacable stillness. Joined in
Non-time and halted in free fall.

xviii

It's all a resurrection song.
Would it ever be got right
The dead could rush home
Keen to press their chinos.

xix

She do the bereaved in different voices
For the point of this address is to prod
And shepherd you back within range
Of my strained ears; extort your reply
By finding any device to hack through
The thickening shades to you, you now
Strangely unresponsive son, who were
Such reliably kind and easy company,
Won't you be summoned up once more
By my prancing and writhing in a dozen
Mawkish modes of reedy piping to you
– Still no? Then let me rest, my dear.

xx

My sisters and my mother,
Weep dark tears for me
I drift as lightest ashes
Under a southern sea

O let me be, my mother
In no unquiet grave
My bone-dust is faint coral
Under the fretful wave

Four blindfolded songs

The hart he's on the hill.
The stout woodpigeon
Sobs her patient measure
From out a muffled shrub.

How neat her gilded eye
Too spare for garlanded
Ornament. Still to be
Marquetry, and to coo.

*

Past avenues of pines
I'll journey to whiteness.
Small wife at the gate
Be mild as is your nature.

Over bristling plains
By six municipalities
Eagerly I'll bounce
Into a thronged arcade,

Lanterns rosy at night
Looped from mossy tiles.
Rounded in lamplight
Thou, gleaming myriad.

*

Dogged brute paddles
To raise its decent *Arf*
Tail streams feathered
And muzzle jutted out.

Bright brown the water
And bright brown the fur
Near drowned the barking
Through coffee liqueur.

*

Glossed ilex, and the olive groves striped
By dry runnels. Resistible. Went wandering
Up and down & all throughout the town
Past its 'spandrels representing the electric
Telegraph'. There may be a tale, though
A song precede it. That woodpigeon
Groans nicely to fan her leaves, yet not to
Keen, though interlaced with briars, though
We think as our lives have led us to think
Or on the whole; though the dusk settles in
Like . . . like a metaphor. Though *though*.

Tree seen from bed

The fuller leaves are ridged, the newer red.
Sunshine is pooled over them, like lacquer.
One branch catches a notion of movement,
shivering, then the rest cotton on in a rush
roused by the wind, to thrash and vacillate.
A toss-up, where they'll all go next – to lash
around through summer until autumn, that
is where; to fall. May it be managed lightly
though it could well turn wilder beforehand.
Tree watched from my sickbed, read to me.
Read from the hymnal of frank life – of how
to be old, yet never rehearse that fact cosily.

There aren't any stories

Once their stories start up, you'll fall silent –
having no family, can offer them nothing,
can't be one for nostalgia, born illegitimate
in those postwar years when it still counted
as seriously shaming – to some, that shame
should be seared onto their child, much as
paper in sunlight, once rays through a lens
are focused hard onto it, can get blackened
and curl up; now attending wholeheartedly
to the others' old anecdotes, you have none
of your own to trade back; there's not much
to tell about having grown up with hatred.
Nor would you want to get branded again,
for those to whom violence was done aren't
fated to hand it down – it's the doctrinaire
sheltered judge who'll insist everyone must;
you grasped that it burned itself out on you.

Late March

Wry day. Winter, of you
we've had enough. And I have
had enough of sniping memory
or strappy agapanthus leaves in sleet
gone orange at their tips, weak leather.
This charged air has a keen and whitish feel
that stings a little, but has gaiety. So, human you,
I'll hand you back to your own camouflage.
Not as 'bleak weather', though. You might.

Pythian

What, put out on the motorway, will lumber twinkling across the lanes of hazard.

The dog's lovability might rub off on it, when it hides in the straw of his kennel.

Sugared the hillocks of retrospective innocence, while acrid the sheer accidents

of a life, or were they. They were. Now yelps ricochet from a monolith, sat deaf

as is true to its nature. It's got nothing for which to atone, it's the very end stone

in a long row of such silences. For 'a wounded spirit who can bear' – *tell* me. If

it *is* through finding your listener that you'd come to grasp your own monologue,

where next could this call turn, massing and purpling as low thunder, though just

whiny to stopped ears; would its *heu* not sink to *phew,* once its weepier appeals tail

off into sepia? No, they'll smoke and foam to whip up a god, or some secular god

who'd be kind to a damp petitioner, but how's her or his correct name made flesh.

Speech-sounds descend, snag in the hair, then flap off to mouth their apostrophes.

A cry reels around, though it's not a Cassandra's but something more speaker-free.

There was and there is a life, I swim in it, but I wouldn't say that it's exactly 'mine'

Clemency

Sweet goose, fat on spring's
fine ideals, hiss in a lime sauce –

clemency's glow is rueful, citrine-
veined, then always ends up being

about practical kindness – don't tut!
That's brilliantly green and airy

& will frogmarch some right round
under the blinking sun so look lively.

In Nice

Where did they get to?
It's untidy without them;
chic or fanned flat, those
house sparrows in teams.
– Pip, sirrah, southbound
to red dust scuffles. To
where the lemon trees.

Still

You're dead but you still flicker bluish – I'd not
want to jinx anyone by bobbing like you do
right in my eye's corner, it's maddening.
Rather turn stolid, go blocky, be granite, not
whirr and not flare but lodge stock-still, a slab.
Not become fish, or a sea, nothing fluid, no darting,
no welling up after my death in the mouths of the living,
those very few concerned. What they'll make of this
coming great lump of myself, who knows, though
let them be easy. Let it keep inert. But may they
bear it untroubled if despite its stone density
something self-driven that no-one could plan for
or fashion or help or screen out or subdue
still puts up its fight to stay animate.

Composed underneath Westminster Bridge

Broad gravel barges shove the drift. Each wake
Thwacks the stone steps. A rearing tugboat streaked
Past moorhens dabbing floss, spun pinkish-beaked.
Peanuts in caramelised burnt chocolate bake
Through syrupy air. Above, fried onions cake.
Pigeons on steeleyed dates neck-wrestled, piqued,
Oblivious to their squabs that whined and squeaked
In iron-ringed nests, nursed in high struts. Opaque
Brown particles swarm churning through the tide.
That navy hoop of cormorant can compose
A counter to this shield – eagles splayed wide,
Gold martlets – on the bridge's side; it glows
While through the eau-de-nil flaked arches slide
The boats 'Bert Prior' and 'The Eleanor Rose'.

Under the answering sky

I can manage being alone,
can pace out convivial hope
across my managing ground.
Someone might call, later.

What do the dead make of us
that we'd flay ourselves trying
to hear them though they may
sigh at such close loneliness.

I would catch, not my echo,
but their guarantee that this
bright flat blue is a mouth
of the world speaking back.

There is no depth to that blue.
It won't 'bring the principle
of darkness with it', but hums
in repose, as radiant static.

'When we cry to Thee'

Stout voyager, put out
to a black sea. I had no
mother, yet still I have
become one. Marine.
I'm sick inside this single
darkness. Inky swell,
carry me. Hymns ancient
& modern, buoy us up
though I am faithless.

'The eclipse'

Acacias domed by a quick breeze into
shivery plumes, bunched then sinking.
Dusk, crossroads, walker, flats, night.
That rapid wordless halt bewilders me.
Now evening will hold still for years.
Fear has clamped on its stiffened face.
It knows what should have been done.
It understood what it turned away from.

A baptism

Lit as near secular,
blackened in filaments,
violet whips up its
rich voices into airily
massed *ah oh ah ohs*
as it stings in divining
some men clumped in
pale muslin by water a
washier blue than the sky
clean as its lanky dove.

Silent did depart

'A spirit casts no shadow' – true, of the filmy dead.
Not of a living creature tapering itself to an obelisk.
Rocky mute, life's too serious for this not speaking!
Don't be stuccoed so hard over any humane seepage.

What had been churning round in that ardent pillar?
You'd not have dreamed an upright man could petrify.
Drape my anointing hair at the feet of superb cement.
All hindsight shakes itself out vigorously like a wet dog.

With Child in mind

And when he came to the
broad river, he took off
his coat and swam. There
were reed beds, whistling.

Smoke. Burning somewhere
on the rainy wind, far
along the sobbing wind.
Get away with you now.

Krasnoye Selo

Below a charcoal sky
leaching the squat houses,
days tighten round each
other as the hours weaken.

Umbrellas and their carriers
go slipping to their tasks.
By dusk they've quickly
dwindled away, got tiny.

Shoes sound so pointed
on their way to nowhere.
Purposefully they'll clop
through the constricted air.

Moving toward my silence
I'll speak evening thoughts
sparkling with reproach though
I had meant to forgive.

Listening for lost people

Still looking for lost people – look unrelentingly.
'They died' is not an utterance in the syntax of life
where they belonged, no *belong* – reanimate them
not minding if the still living turn away, casually.
Winds ruck up its skin so the sea tilts from red-blue
to blue-red: into the puckering water go his ashes
who was steadier than these elements. Thickness
of some surviving thing that sits there, bland. Its
owner's gone nor does the idiot howl – while I'm
unquiet as a talkative ear. Spring heat, a cherry
tree's fresh bronze leaves fan out and gleam – to
converse with shades, yourself become a shadow.
The souls of the dead are the spirit of language:
you hear them alight inside that spoken thought.

After 'Nous n'irons plus au bois'

We've had it with the woods.
The underbrush got felled.
Grab who you want, now
that there's no more cover.
None left for a cicada. Do
we let that beauty leap and
see her thump the ground
we'd cleared of dying laurel?
Sweet-throated warbler, yelp.
Off trots the she-shepherd
with a basket for briar roses
or strawberries, should the
churned earth house them.

Orphic

I've lived here dead for decades – now you
pitch up gaily among us shades, with your
freshly dead face all lit up, beaming – but
after my long years without you, don't think
it will be easy. It's we dead who should run
whispering at the heels of the living, yet you
you'd put the frighteners on me, ruining
the remains of your looks in bewailing me
not handling your own last days with spirit.
Next you'll expect me to take you around
introducing some starry goners. So mother
do me proud and hold your white head high.
On earth you tried, try once again in Hades.

'I told it not'

Tap, in this bland October
that cedar's ripening cones
piped pinkish green along
its lower branches, tap until
their pollen spills to writhe
in bright lime powder coils.
This frankly panto jealousy
makes it such a lurid tree.

Following Heine

I cried in my sleep as I thought
you were in your grave, I woke but
went on weeping. I dreamt you'd
abandoned me, I woke to cry bitterly.
I slept. In my sleep, I wept as I
dreamt you were still good to me.
I awoke in unrelenting tears.

And another thing

Some new arrival's coming, whose name may not be happy.
Attend it. Childishly lovely, once, to listen to anyone new
as if even the oldest harm was outgrown as a liberty bodice.
Does sifting through damage ease, or enshrine it; how grasp
a past, but not skid on embittered accounting? The ledgers
exhibit their black surplus malice and red lack of tenderness,
while 'suffering' easily gets competitive as each suspects hers
was the rougher lot, yet feels shy out of shame at her history
that won't dovetail with her present. Hoist personalised flags
though they're so stiff with encrusted blood they'd first need
a good sousing in tears? – forget that. Could the years have
been easier if you'd just settled early on hating a sex instead,
although which one of them to begin with? Sleeked up your
plumes to swan out and ruffle your usual vexers of dailiness?
Filed reports to the muses, via cicadas' surveillance, on men
who weren't rapt, only dozing in warm grass at noon, lulled
by music to dreaming their sonic enchantment is virtuously
militant, a sparkly art stance plus a strong civic end in itself?
It's late. 'You must live as you can', which is all we ever did.

Boxy piece

Exhibit of small boxes made from wood
to house their thought and each an open
coffin of the not-dead with their chirring.
Satin-lined frames stack square in blocks
nested to a columbarium – then mumble
closet doves, whose fond carpenter drills
piercings for more air, won't let you flap.

Catastrophic thinking

It willed to be ordinary, easy
as rain sifting through woods
but doubt shrouded that mind
skewing its aim at mildness.

Fires were lit and sap hissed
in young branches torn down
by anxiety contorted to shield
itself, biting its angry hands.

It smoked out each transparent joy.
It strode well away from its heart.
Darkness absorbs any mind, once
it starts calling itself 'unwanted'.

The patient who had no insides

i The ins and outs of it

As clouds swell to damply fill gaps in mountains, so in
Illness we sense, solidly, our entrails expanding to stuff
That space of our innerness just feebly imagined before.

I'd slumped at home before the nightly documentaries
Of scalpels nipping through the primrose fat, beaded
With that orange hue that blood becomes on camera,

But only when they crossly assert themselves do those
Guts I hadn't believed in, truly come home in me.
Figuratively, yes, we've guts – literally, may suspect

We haven't – poking sceptical as Doubting Thomases
For what's packed below skin we don't see laid bare.
Invaginated folds, ballooning orifices, we know about

And pregnancy, watching some unborn other's heels
Nudging and butting like carp snouts under the navel.
That's someone else altogether, palpable inside me.

No, it's my disbelief in my own entrails that I mean.
I'd glimpsed the radiographer's dark film, starring
Barium-whitened swags of colon, mine. Blown glass,

Hooped entrails ridged with their glazed diverticules
Like little suckers studded plumply on squid tentacles
Of my intestines. But now I see their outer evidence:

My ginger skin. How well you look, they'd said to me
At work. But no tan browned my face. The malady
Conveyed an air of robust health through bronzing me.

ii On the ward of signs and humours

Now foamy bracken-brown urine cools in plastic jugs
For measuring on the ward, frothed like a hillside stream
Relaxing into pools. 'What says the doctor to my water?'

Jaundice is read as if the humours still remained reliable.
There were insides inside me – now they've gone all wrong.
Modern regimes of signs set in, and newly prudent thoughts

That what they stamp, we own. Pointers to a depth, to be
'Philosophically, Medicinally, Historically open'd & cut up'.
From Burton's ripe account of melancholy, that last quote.

The sorrows brood inside our purplish spleens, barriers
That check dark moods of sultry bile by segregating it
Where it can't seep to hurt us. Anatomised emotion.

'Pancreas' means 'all flesh'. Now, awry, it chews itself.
That piece of ambient meat I am eats meaty me all up.
Enzymes flood to champ their host, their prey – that's

Me. They don't know where to stop. I'm auto-gesting.
Spontaneous combustion in a schlock Victorian engraving
Of hearthrug scorched, charred ankles jutting out of boots,

No more of faithful Lizzie left. A hapless autophage I am
Whose fizzog has gone bad. Enzymes digesting tissue grind
In rampant amylase and swollen lipase counts. Sure signs

Affecting the liver, a plush nursery for the vegetal spirit.
Fondly this warming organ clasps the stomach set over it
Fingering heat into it, nursing its charge, so Galen held.

Flame-like, this liver, slow-cooking the stomach's stuff
Down to a bloodlike juice. Not boiling it dry to char it
Or simmering it to gruel – if the liver's temper is right.

Noble the strong liver, 'dark monarch' to Neruda.
But ignoble, the long slim pear of the gall bladder
And the sole-like spleen, roughened, its shoe shape

Splayed into an ox tongue. Spleen, milky-pulped
Innocent home to the darkest of humours, frees all
Merriment in its bearer, by holding black bile apart

And so, wrote Harvey, 'the spleen causes one to laugh'.
Dreaming of red things, the sanguine man keeps bluff,
Night dreads held safely at bay. Splenetic laughter!

'Remembering mine affliction and my misery
The wormwood and the gall.' So cries Lamentations
Too harsh on the house of that yellow emulsifier,

Hard too on wormwood – a friend, boiled to absinthe,
To smoky Verlaine, and the maker of Pernod's fortune.
Antique are that shrubby vermifuge's properties: bitter

Carminative, anthelmintic, cholagogue, febrifuge,
Swelling the secretion of both liver and gall bladder.
Bluish or red-brown skin markings today? Bad signs.

iii *The patient longs to know*

Back on the ward, the darting housemen, veering,
Swerve low by ends of beds like swifts, but then zoom off.
Come back! the impatient patient wails, though silently,

Why am I 'nil by mouth' for endless days? Am I each day
Prepped for some other op which never comes – or what?
Unreadable as a leaving lover, no houseman stops to say.

'Your notes got lost so we might send you back, pre-op.
Without your write-up, no, the anaesthetist won't like it.'
My starved heart sinks at hearing this; it's bodily starved

Like all the rest of me, so long on 'nil by mouth'. Nil
In my own mouth, yes, to eat or drink – but also nil
Issued as word of explanation from a doctor's mouth.

Let me go home so I can find things out. Googling
Fulfils the nineteenth century's dream of ardent enquiry
Amassed, and nearly democratically. On medics' sites

The grand Miltonic phrases of the biliary tract race home:
Islets of Langerhans, Ampulla of Vater, Duct of Santorini,
Sphincter of Oddi. Sonorous names, some the narrowings

Which, blocked, can cause grave trouble. They had for me;
That gall bladder, choked, must go. But will its ghost
Kick up in me, once it is tossed away? This oddness of

Owning spare parts. Our bodies littered with redundancies,
Walking reliquaries rattling our appendices, blunt tails,
Primordial. For we are birds with teeth and empty crops.

iv The consultant summarises our national health

'Liver, until so recently the Cinderella of medicine!
Just the girl in the clinical ashes, unrescued as yet
Assailed by her bad suitors – weak policies and folly.

'Alcohol-led liver failure rising, bile duct cancer rates
Mounting, more cirrhosis from viral illness, Hep B, C.
More drinking, younger drinking, increased steatosis,

'Yet funders don't cough up for self-induced sickness.
Specialists get scarcer, beds vanish, bureaucracy swells
As need begs for new transplants, more artificial livers.

'One gets despondent. Lifestyle's the problem,' adds
This eminent hepatologist, despondent at 'patching up
Self-harming patients, worsened by government policy'.

His time is short. This patient nods and leaves. So
It's our national fantasy, not just my private idiocy,
That what our daily intake is by mouth has nil effect?

v Discharged

'Your liver tests are squiffy, Mrs R, but you might
As well go home, you won't get well in here' – then
He's darted off again, mercurial houseman. Outside
The well ones all charge past us like young bullocks,
Amazingly confident. Those who were ill go gingerly.
A smack of post-ward colour shoves us back to life.

Hiding in plain sight

I try to find you, yet you are not here.
I've studied absence, fought to fill it in –
courage comes easier with a grasp of why.

A secret's camouflaged when unconcealed.
I chose to not see/saw the thing too near?
Absence turns thicker, muscled by its strain.

A moon in daylight, whitest blue on blue,
surprises briefly, to appear surreal
until it slips to rights. I couldn't spot

the obvious – *obviam*, in the way; plain
sight goes blind through chasing clarity.
I looked for you, so couldn't see you gone.

I sensed your not-there in its burning life.
I listened out to feel its silence beat.
It does not speak with any human mouth.

Lines starting with La Rochefoucauld

'It is more shameful to distrust your friends
than be deceived by them': things in themselves
do hold – a pot, a jug, a jar, Sweet Williams'
greenshank shins – so that your eye's pulled
clear of metallic thought by the light constancy
of things, that rest there with you. Or without.
That gaily deadpan candour draws you on.
Your will to hope quickens in their muteness.

Oh go away for now

Persistent are your lost or dead
intimates and buried child.

They won't leave their wants unsaid
but tag you with appeals and prods

while your 'work of mourning' quails
before each sibilant attack

inveigling you to lead them back:
'You've loved us terribly, and so

you've kept us going, even though . . .'
Calmly heap fresh soil upon them.

They can wait for you to join them
as soon you will; you'll soon gang up

to poke and give some new grief to
whoever, left living, once loved you.

On the Black Isle

Three ginger temples of oil rigs clamped at the bay's mouth, a
big navy sky roiled over cloud pillars; the notebook goes riffling
through its colour chart for rose-flushed stonework cut clean as
these rain-beaded fuchsias or until that notebook, a mental one,
flips round to enquire whitely: *Just what do you think you're up to?*
'Any gay thing's worth a chase, for as long as its shade distracts –
so drape, far rain, hung in cinematic swathes.' Its next reproach
isn't appealing, either: *So where am I in this?* 'We aren't – this is in
rosy Cromarty, its broad fields racing by and silvery ruthless rain
nettling our scoured skins.' – Quite vanished, and never said why.
Thick kelp straps gleam in the shallows and loll on the rising tide.

'They saw you coming'

I don't resemble my face.
Once it had looked like me.
Who'd have seriously thought
Damage would pounce again.
No, nothing ever gets learnt.
Some slaps and yet another
Bright blind sunshiny day.
Maybe that's as well, since
Experience deduces in tears
The odds-on return of harm.
Better then not to study
Its adamant heartsick brief.

A man 'was stood' there

On pitted sand the urchin shards fan out, but the watcher's
braced in shingle, wet grit scraping around ankles rammed
in an undertow, wrack fronds whipped on skin as he senses
himself raced faster than pebbles grinding toward the rising
water, while his feet stream out behind him in a moonwalk.
You'd get rushed backwards just by standing still, he'll muse
catching a tiniest roaring underfoot – but what thought does
he find in that sound, or purely his dizziness on being rolled
away from the sea, as one lost to his naturally rocky balance
that he'll recalibrate now at the core of a man 'being stood'.

Percy's Relique;
on the Death of John Hall's Peacock

Earl Percy of Brook Mill, in gown
Of brown with azure trimmings, flown!

Grand and admired fowl, indenturing
John your janitor to toss you copious nuts,

Rare! Raoaark! Rare! You were adornment.
You were Brook Mill. Its visitors were yours.

You Shelley to us duller poets, Percy. Flare!
Go, glittering! Your fan recalls you from her desk

Lamenting, where our London peafowls droop
And sigh for iridescent Percy and his shrieks.

An awkward lyric

It sits with itself in its arms. Out of
the depth of its shame it starts singing
a hymn of pure shame, surging in the throat.
To hold a true note could be everything.
Getting the hang of itself would undo it.

Cardiomyopathy

Unlovely meaty thing, a heart – unlikeliest
'seat of the affections'. Indifferent to its human
wrapper, the brute pigheaded muscle wallops on.
It is a pump, impersonal in its lub-dup shunt.
But it can be a pump that stops itself, if its cells
have grown awry, like toppled pancakes; that
kind of heart will get too big for its own good.
Self-sabotage, on auto-pilot, starts to fatten it.
Its septum thickens silently as the thing slogs on
about its idiot work of self-enlargement, or until
its motor limps and a surprise arrhythmia makes
it choke and stagger like a flooding carburettor
while its electrics race, then quiver, then go still.
I've had to work this out alone. I'm sounding
too forensic? – but you'll go on with your dead,
go as far as you can; that's why my imagination
wouldn't wait outside the morgue, but burst in
to half-anaesthetise itself with knowing; as I was
the witness to his start as an ivory and ice-blue
newborn cyanosed by my long labour, sliced out
by caesarean, so I did try to keep him company
even after the end, when his too-big heart got
flopped down on a metal tray to bare the weak
fold in its mitral valve, and the glossy cling-film
of lilac membranes coating its large ventricles –
I can't quite leave the autopsy room for good.

My living on indicts me. If my own heart
contracted briefly, it still pushed on past yours.

Hearts, being muscular, power on as they can.
Mine was relentless in outpacing yours.

'The heart is a hard flesh, not easily injured'
so Galen wrote. He bypassed those like yours.

My heart, though old, seems tough enough and so
I would have gladly had it changed, for yours.

There is heart failure, and however well we mean,
the failure's mutual; though the worse loss is yours.

Touristic in Kyoto

Irises, by a pond freckled with spring waterweed.
Hiding from the wind, an onlooker dabs away
to get herself clean out of the picture,
leaving no colour note.
Better, no picture – certainly
no 'thin rain of blossom'.

Little Eva

Time took your love – now time will take its time.
'Move on', you hear, but to what howling emptiness?
The kinder place is closest to your dead
where you lounge in confident no-motion, no thought
of budging. Constant in analytic sorrow, you abide.
It even makes you happy when you're feeling blue.
Jump up, jump back. Flail on the spot.
I can disprove this 'moving-on' nostrum.
Do the loco-motion in my living room.

This poem contains brief excerpts from the lyrics to 'The Loco-Motion',
words and music by Gerry Goffin and Carole King, originally performed
by Eva Boyd as Little Eva.

Never to disinter the pink companion

Never to disinter the pink companion. Wintry. So isn't everyone
drawn to human warmth, if only by animal curiosity? Seems not.
Then how pleasantly to give back his enigma of wordless absence
to its real owner, like a jacket he'd not realised he'd left behind?
Worse, he had: 'Thanks a lot for another trip to the charity shop.'
To confess my bafflement with grace. So, tolerant Grace, though
I've needed to call for you so often, please don't ignore my knocks
but uncoil from your couch and ease out of your door, smiling, to
me mulish with a little scar literature, it is a very late form of love.

Let no air now be sung

Let no air now be sung, let no kind air –
sorrow alone reveals a constant pulse.
A trusted oak deceives the pliant back
coiled into it like a fern shoot aping an
archbishop's crook held high as a truth
paraded through hazy woods in its veil
to get snapped off by that wild anxiety
figuring its jail could be quit in a slash
clean down to her dear bone – it wills
to twitch its hem aside and motor on.
Let no air now be sung, let no kind air.

'I admit the briar'

I admit the briar.
The grave rose knots it,
both coiled about in shade.

A padded heart draws barbs —
worked free, they won't make
relics however buffed up.

Full of wist, I needn't be.
The fuller world's not 'cruel' to me
more like indifferent —

I am that world. What was it
Flora Tristan cried
in her corkscrew gaiety:

'When I behold Thy crown of thorns,
Thy bitter trials, O Lord, how trivial
do they seem compared to mine!'

You men who go in living flesh

You men who go in living flesh
Scour clean then drape your souls
In plumy dress that they may rise
Clear of those thrashing shoals

Of mackerel of the sea who call
You loiterers on the strand
To heed your future salted lungs
Pegged out to dry on sand.

I was upright upon the field
Another thing in the sea.
Its light has washed my eyelids shut.
Green grass floats over me.

Hope is an inconsistent joy
Yet blazes to renew
Its lambent resurrections of
Those gone ahead of you.

Death makes dead metaphor revive

Death makes dead metaphor revive,
Turn stiffly bright and strong.
Time that is felt as 'stopped' will freeze
Its to-fro, fro-to song

I parrot under feldspar rock
Sunk into chambered ice.
Language, the spirit of the dead,
May mouth each utterance twice.

Spirit as echo clowns around
In punning repartee
Since each word overhears itself
Laid bare, clairaudiently.

An orphic engine revs but floods
Choked on its ardent weight.
Disjointed anthems dip and bob
Down time's defrosted spate.

Over its pools of greeny melt
The rearing ice will tilt.
To make *rhyme* chime again with *time*
I sound a curious lilt.

'A gramophone on the subject'

1 *The postwar exhumation squad's verses*

Exhumation squads dug to unearth them
In bits that got dropped in cloth bags
While one man stood by with his notebook
Recording all readable tags.

It was not the most popular service
Retracing those old trench charts
Then shaking off well-rotted khaki
From almost unknowable parts.

One father pitched up to bribe us
To hand him a charred scrap of shirt.
He'd worked out it was his son there.
We told him the thing was just dirt.

Blood mud had thickened to rich mud
Which settled as grassed-over clay.
Matching pieces with names wasn't easy
Despite what 'their' new headstones say.

2 'It isn't catching, you know'

Those of a tender conscience swear
Their vows that they will fail to keep.
At the first whiff of human need
Each scatters like a panicked sheep.

You had believed that some might stay,
So earnestly they'd sworn they would.
Without one word they slipped away
To save themselves – that's understood.

When each in turn gets hit by loss
Who but himself will cluster round.
A black joke – 'mutual empathy' –
To faces set like hardened ground.

3 'If any question why'

We do not draw our curtains closed.
We're told we should not mind
This change from custom; our old way
Would make whole streets look blind.

What all this means may yet come clear.
Telegrams, at more doors, 'regret'.
You can't ask what's the good of it.
Their names might get in the *Gazette*.

4 'Tucked in where they fell'

'Tucked in' is not quite how we'd put it.
We weren't plumped up neatly in bed.
If you 'fell' as one piece you were lucky,
Not dismembered before you were dead.

We wore dog-tags of vulcanised fibre
But those need their dog to stay whole
Or to keep enough bone to be tied on
Not be draped off some tree in a scroll.

Had we managed to get home living
We'd trouble you worse than the dead.
Shambling, like blind men, among you
And most probably gone in the head.

So we've formed our heavenly choir
Composed of our melded limbs.
Each voices his part in the singing.
We can't disentangle our hymns.

We get noisy as larks in the sunshine.
Your leg's with his head over there.
My fist's stuck upright from a dugout
And it's clutching a hank of his hair.

5 'Their Name Liveth For Evermore'

Death's tidied up in rows and lists.
The scratched are 'Known to God'.
'He is not missing: he is here' –
Else in the awkward squad.

His name's got weightier than him.
He's been peeled off from it.
It didn't much suit him in his life.
That went AWOL. Poor fit.

What is it for some name to 'live'?
It's lifeless. Set in stone.
Its bearer proved too slight for it.
He'd always been 'Unknown'.

6 'Death of a Hero'

'I droop', it pales, 'like a solitary wood anemone'.
But they're surrounded by their white-faced friends
and each of them gets wind-whipped – then, solitary
as an unpretty thing lamenting *help me*, if too quietly.
It is the painted mouth gurning behind its bars. Best
if it forgets to be ham, or plant, or to have attributes.

7 'He lies somewhere in France'. Somewhere.

What can it mean, that someone walks
out of your house then they won't come

back ever. When you'd had them, and
they were boys; you'd think they'd make

their own way home out of that mud.
He was like a cat, always fell on his feet.

I can feel he's still working in the fields
or is drinking late somewhere – oh I do

know that he's not & yet none of it fits.
Then what could it mean to *know* this.

We learnt that the line between here
and there is a faint grey, and it gleams

like the honesty's seedpods – as brittle.
But candid somehow. Hard to convey

how it seems fresh, and almost papery.
You could poke a hole and be straight

through onto the death side, where it
is livelier than here, and a lot clearer.

I never could grasp human absence.
It always escaped me, the real name

of this unfathomable simplest thing.
It's his hands I remember the most.

But that'll go. Some women take on
a wary look and seem bleached out.

They get pierced by a casual remark
that makes them harden or go vague.

'I fought for strength and tearlessness
and found both.' What price, pride.

No need to draw attention to yourself.
So many were left as quiet as you. Do

I go on for years thinking and thinking.
One in all these thousands. Him. Me.

So many gone that you can't take it in.
Whatever I say is bound to sound flat.

I am a gramophone on the subject.
Each day's same horizon to be faced.

You long to fade out into it, yourself.
I look doggedly after a missing figure.

What to do now is clear, and wordless.
You will bear what can not be borne.

ACKNOWLEDGEMENTS

Some of these poems first appeared online, or in paper form, in *Blackbox Manifold* [2013]; *Intercapillary Space* [2013, 2014]; *Snow* [2013]; *English* [2015]; *Constitutional Information* [2015]; *Poetry London* [2014]; *Poetry Ireland Review* [2015]; *Earth Has Not Any Thing to Shew More Fair: A Bicentenary Celebration of Wordsworth's 'Sonnet Composed Upon Westminster Bridge'* [The Wordsworth Trust and Shakespeare's Globe, 2002]; *London Review of Books* [2012]; *Signs and Humours: The Poetry of Medicine* [Calouste Gulbenkian Foundation, 2007]; *The Pity* [The Poetry Society, 2014]; *Translation Games* [Arts and Humanities Research Council, 2015]; *Zone* [2013]; *Shearsman 97 & 98* [2013/2014]; *UEA LDC Poetry Reading Series* [Eggbox, 2014].

I thank all the editors and publishers concerned, including those who commissioned some of this work.

The collection's title is taken from W. S. Graham's 'Implements in their Places' in *New Collected Poems: W. S. Graham*, ed. Matthew Francis [Faber and Faber, London, 2004, p.247].

Notes to the poems

In 'Four blindfolded songs' the spandrels are by George Frampton, on Electra House, 84 Moorgate, London.

'Composed under Westminster Bridge' has in mind Wordsworth's 'Composed Upon Westminster Bridge'. It was commissioned for *Earth Has Not Any Thing to Shew More Fair: A Bicentenary Celebration of Wordsworth's 'Sonnet Composed Upon Westminster Bridge'*, The Wordsworth Trust and Shakespeare's Globe, 2002.

'The eclipse' follows the closing scene of Michelangelo Antonioni's 1962 film, *L'Eclisse*.

'A baptism' refers to Piero della Francesca's 'The Baptism of Christ' in the National Gallery, London.

'Following Heine' draws on Heinrich Heine's 'Ich hab' im Traum geweinet' from his *Lyric Intermezzo*.

NOTES TO 'The patient who had no insides'
These are taken from my sequence commissioned for *Signs and Humours, The Poetry of Medicine*, edited by Lavinia Greenlaw, Calouste Gulbenkian Foundation, London 2007. I'm grateful to Professor Roger Williams for his observations, relayed in section iv.
  Falstaff, in *Henry IV, Part 1*, asks 'What says the doctor to my water?'
  The subtitle of Robert Burton's *Anatomy of Melancholy*, 1621, includes 'Philosophically, Medicinally, Historically open'd and cut up'.

Galen, c. AD 200, describes the liver as clasping and warming the stomach to cook its contents. He held that the gall bladder, spleen and liver produced and stored three of the four bodily humours; yellow bile, black bile, and sanguine.

Pablo Neruda wrote an 'Ode to the Liver', 1956.

In 1635 William Harvey termed the liver a noble organ, but the spleen ignoble, describing it as like an ox tongue or a sole of a foot.

In Nicholas Culpeper's *Astrological Judgement of Diseases from the Decumbiture of the Sick*, 1655, the sanguine man 'dreameth of red things'.

Wormwood as a remedy for digestive ills included absinthe, which was manufactured by Henri-Louis Pernod in 1797.

The 'bad signs' of rampaging enzymes in severe acute pancreatitis include bluish and reddish-brown skin discolouration.

'Percy's Relique; on the Death of John Hall's Peacock' imitates Wallace Stevens' poem 'Bantams in Pine-Woods'.

'I admit the briar' was commissioned by *Poetry Ireland Review* for the 150th anniversary of Yeats' birth. It begins with the first line of W. B. Yeats' poem 'A First Confession' in his 'A Woman Young and Old'.

Notes to 'A Gramophone on the Subject'

These verses come from my sequence 'A gramophone on the subject' in *The Pity* [The Poetry Society, 2014], commissioned as part of a commemoration in poetry of the 1914–1918 war. They draw on historical records, including soldiers' and civilians' letters, diaries and memoirs.

1 The postwar exhumation squad's verses
Bodies were often destroyed beyond recognition, after repeated bombardment. The 'exhumation squads' were soldiers who did the work of

disinterring already buried remains from the battlefields, for reburial in the new military cemeteries nearby. They'd note any intact identification tags. Occasionally some determined parents would travel to where the exhumation squads were working and try to get hold of their son's remains to take home. They were supposed to be stopped from doing this.

2 *'It isn't catching, you know'*
These lines voice the darkly sensitised thoughts of the contemporary bereaved about the tendency of some to avoid them. What lasting silences might have set in after 1914–1918, when thousands had died, but when public religious commemoration often took the form of respecting their 'national sacrifice'? In her 'A Sketch of the Past', Virginia Woolf wrote 'That is one of the aspects of death which is left out when people talk of the message of sorrow: they never mention its unbecoming side: its legacy of bitterness, bad temper, ill adjustment.'

3 *'If any question why'*
The wearing of black armbands, the closing of household curtains after a death, and other mourning rituals were gradually abandoned after the start of the 1914–1918 war. The *'Gazette'* is *The London Gazette*, in which details of those who'd been awarded military service medals were published, often posthumously. My title comes from Rudyard Kipling's couplet, 'If any question why we died/ Tell them, because our fathers lied.'

4 *'Tucked in where they fell'*
These verses could be sung by dead soldiers replying to Edwin Lutyens, one of the main war cemetery architects. He was visiting the Ypres battle sites when he wrote this description in a letter home: 'a ribbon of isolated graves like a milky way across miles of country where men were tucked in where they fell.'

5 *'Their Name Liveth For Evermore'*
This wording appeared on many war memorials. How to name and record

the dead of 1914–1918 was a strikingly prominent question. The ideal of dignifying those lost beyond any hope of burial produced the emblematic figure of the Unknown Soldier. 'Their Name Liveth For Evermore' was engraved on many war memorials including the Menin Gate at Ypres. This monument invoked another, would-be consoling, rubric; 'He is not missing; he is here.' My speakers offer their own laconic thoughts on this matter of names without bodies, bodies without names.

6 *'Death of a Hero'*

A note on post war aesthetic isolation, as if by some 'modernist' writer: *Death of a Hero* is the title of Richard Aldington's 1929 novel about the unhappy return of a disenchanted soldier.

7 *'He lies somewhere in France'. Somewhere.*

The phrase 'He lies somewhere in France' often indicated an untraceable body. What do you do when you have no body to bury, and you're also well aware that your own loss is the tiniest part of a global catastrophe? Arthur Conan Doyle wrote 'All that I can do is be a gramophone on the subject', referring to his spiritualist conviction of the reality of contact with the war dead. The line 'I fought for strength and tearlessness and found both' is from a diary entry by Alda, Lady Hoare, made during her son's last leave before he was killed. It's in her manuscript 'This Short Sketch of the Life of Our Son', 1916.